HONICKNOWLE REMEMBERED

Arthur L. Clamp

HONICKNOWLE WEEK 1937

Each year they have such a fine time,
In the village of Honicknowle.
Now I'll try to put it in rhyme,
Now how shall I start? I know.

Now first of all there is the "Queen"
With her attendants, so sweet and refine,
Three such girls you never have seen,
Oh! How I wish they were mine.

Full praise must go to Ed. Lewis
And all his committee so good,
Without them they could not do this,
There's no one who possibly could.

The crowning takes place on the Monday
Inside the Village Hall
But pardon me, first on the Sunday,
The service starts rolling the ball.

On Tuesday comes the children's parade.
In dresses all made by themselves,
The costumes are certainly well made,
To resemble boxers, kings, pixies and elves.

Tuesday evening is the football match,
The women, they kick and they prance,
The Honicknowle team is right up to scratch,
This being followed by a dance.

Now Wednesday is the day of the fayre,
With stalls all lined in a row
Pretty ladies all selling their ware
No matter wherever you go.

Wednesday evening is the night of nights,
The people flock from all parts,
They all want to see the sights,
The cycles, the motor cars and carts.

Thursday is the night for the men.
The night of boxing and wrestling,
Just one fatal punch, and then
In the ambulance they will be nestling.

There's a dance again on the Friday,
And each girl is there with her man.
They're all wound up for the cabaret,
By Miss Lamb's famous *Can, Cans*.

On Saturday there is no ending to fun,
There's sports, fireworks and dancing. Oh! Boy!
By the time that the clock has struck one
Everybody's bubbling over with joy.

Now this poem it may seem so funny,
But it's really an appeal to you.
Don't forget they need the money,
Come on, let's see what you can do.

Author of poem not known.

This version of the book is virtually as originally published.
There are now additional pages at the back providing information about the author.

The republishing project is being managed by Arthur's grandson, Steven Gibson. We aim to find all the research that he was involved in publishing, preserving it for the next generation as part of 'The Clamp Collection'.

INTRODUCTION

THIS illustrated booklet covering much of the life of the one time separate village of Honicknowle is mainly concerned with the last decades before the large scale developments commenced in the 1950s and radically changed the face of the locality. It is hoped that it will be an appropriate record of at least some of the well known events and people featured in the year by year calendar of events.

The village is now part of the large northern area of Plymouth but the map below will show quite another scene not all those many years ago. Like other communities largely left to their own entertainments a surprising number of interesting programmes of events were put together by local people. The outstanding event for Honicknowle was the annual carnival led by the energetic Edgar Lewis which attracted thousands of people from all over the city. It was an event to be well remembered.

The lists of people and occupations in this booklet give some indication of the many activities which took place here. There was also the large Woodland Fort which housed troops from time to time, families and recreational activities. Farming was, of course, the main pursuit with employment at the brickworks and in the Dockyard close runners. The village even had a ropewalk where Mr. T. Palmer made ropes for the Barbican fishermen.

Many people have kindly loaned photographs and gave of their time by recalling childhood memories. I am specially indebted to Mrs. A. Knight (Agnes Lewis) of Weston-super-Mare for supplying albums of prints and newspaper articles and to Miss Smith, Mrs. L. Foster, Mrs. M. Chapman, Mrs. W. Ingle, Mr. R. Palmer, Mrs. R. Scott, Mr. and Mrs. C. Hurst, Mr. Coles, Mrs. E. Cock, Mrs. Tozer, Mrs. Lee and Mrs. C. Angove. Various other people have added information and my thanks are recorded to them all.

Arthur L. Clamp,
203 Elburton Road,
Plymstock, Plymouth

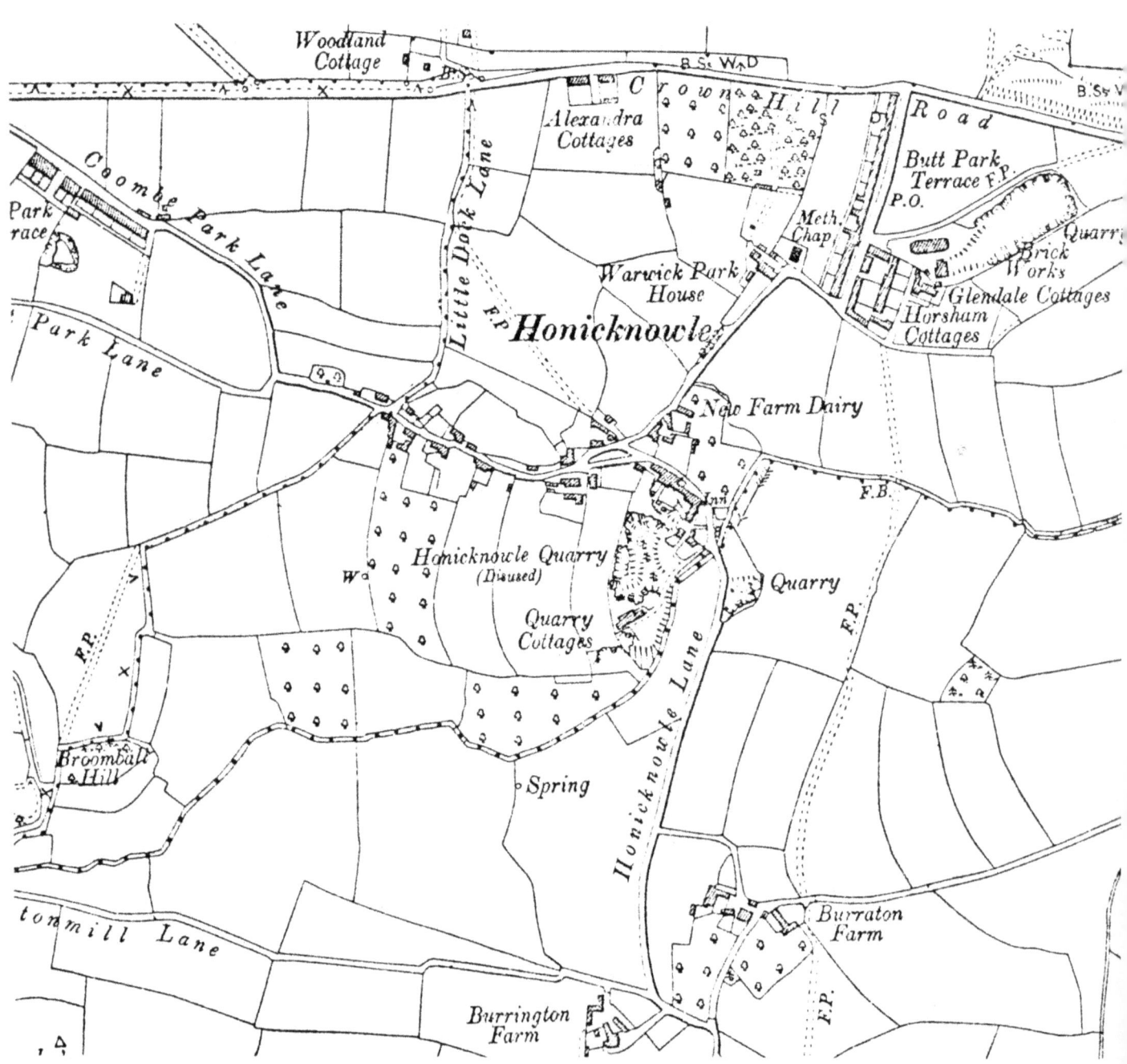

ENTRIES DOUBLED.

HONICKNOWLE SHOW'S SUCCESS

Honicknowle Reading and Recreation Association, which has added a horticultural show to its many activities, has reason to congratulate itself on the success of the exhibition held on Saturday. The entries were double those of last year, the quality was pronounced by the judges to be very good indeed, while the competition in most of the classes was keen. In addition to the display of flowers and vegetables there were numerous attractions, including a parade of children in fancy dress, a baby show which drew many entries, races for children, bowling for a live pig, and, as a final, fireworks. Fine weather favoured the event, and there was a large attendance.

Mrs. H. D. Gill, who was introduced by the president, Mr. W. C. Gingell, and presented with a bouquet by Doris Lewis, opened the show with a little speech, in which she said it was a happy thing to increase the love of gardens, and the friendly rivalry of shows was of the utmost value. The success which attended the event was largely due to the effort of the committee, of which Mr. E. Evans was chairman, Mr. T. Blacker vice-chairman, Mr. H. Tucker hon. treasurer, Mr. E. Lewis hon. secretary, and Mr. R. Hodge assistant secretary. The judges of the flowers and vegetables were Mr. J. Crocker, Plymouth, and Mr. W. Bennett, Plympton; and Mr. H. J. German, St Budeaux, judged the wild flowers, of which there was a good collection. Dr. S. Noy Scott was judge of the baby show, and was assisted by Mrs. Cole and Mrs. Bunn, of the St. John Ambulance. Mrs. W. C. Gingell and Mr. Tucker were judges of the fancy dress.

Aug. 1925

In the open classes of the horticultural show W. R. Atwill was first for plants in pots, asters, coleus, ferns, roses, and pansies, second for geraniums, and third for asters, cactus dahlias, and vegetable marrows. W. H. Jeffery was first for geraniums, bouquets, zinnias, second for coleus, carnations, sweet peas, pansies, and peas, third for plants in pots and carrots. T. Palmer first for dahlias, pompones and cactus, and cabbages, second for asters, roses, zinnias, cucumbers, and won the special for best collection. H. C. Weeks first for stocks, second for ferns, bouquets, and cabbages, third for geraniums and runner beans. A. T. Gray second for dahlias (pompones), and third for ferns. T. Gleave first for asters and sweet peas, second for runner beans, onions, and parsnips. J. Brown first for carrots, runner beans, and cucumber, second for asters and vegetable marrows, third for onions. H. Peard second for plants in pots, third for bouquets. H. D. Gill first for vegetable marrows, second for carrots. J. Sparrow first for onions.

In the cottagers' classes prizewinners were W. R. Atwill, R. Harris, W. Soady, W. H. Jeffery, H. C. Weeks, A. J. Welch, M. Parsons, W. Antis, H. May, A. T. Gray, S. Nichols, S. Fairweather, F. Redding, W. Gray, J. Elliot, J. Sparrow, F. Summers, T. Thomas, A. B. Horn, S. Hodge, and A. A. Shazell. The president's prize for the best collection went to W. R. Harris.

Eggs, brown—1, W. Gray; 2, T. Cleave; 3, W. R. Atwill. White—1, W. J. Gray; 2, H. E. Brown; 3, W. Gray. Potatoes, cooked—1, Mrs. M. Allen; 2, Mrs. E. Palmer; 3, Mrs. A. Lewis.

Wild flowers, under 10—1, Hilda Pearn; 2, Marjorie Kingwell; 3, Dora Lewis. Over 10—1, L. Brown; 2, Winnie Pearn; 3, Winnie Jenkins. Special for greatest number of varieties—Marjorie Bowden.

In the baby show the awards were:—Under 6 months—1, Douglas Sherrell; 2, Sydney Yard; 3, Donald Fleming. Under 12 months—1, Cecil Brown; 2, Joan Smith; 3, Peter Betty. Under 2 years—1, Charles Atwill; 2, Hazel Palmer; 3, Betty Hooper.

Fancy dress, villagers—1, J. Pearce and R. Proude; 2, D. Snell; 3, A. Lewis. Open—1, F. Hocking; 2, B. Bird; 3, B. Betty.

Honicknowle, 1903

Matthews, Henry, Warwick Park
Stephens, Mrs. Annie
Baker, James, Farmer
Butland, Alfred, Farmer, Coombe Farm
Cole, William, Baker, 17 Butt Park Terrace
Daniel, W. T., Woodland Fort Inn
Dennis, Mrs. Shopkeeper, 1 Butt Park Terrace
Holl, H. Agent
Hortop, John F., Dairyman
Lamerton, Thos., Bootmaker, 9 Butt Park Terrace
Langworthy, Geo., Market Gardener
Luke, James, Shopkeeper
Matthews, Henry, Farmer
Oliver, Mrs. I., 19/20 Butt Park Terrace
Palmer, Thos., Ropemaker
Pengelly, John, General Shop, Butt Park Terrace
Perry, Mrs. C., Shopkeeper
Rowe, J., Wood and Coal Dealer
Seldom, Wm., General Shop
Shute, T. Haulier, 3 Horsham Cottages
Snell, Henry, Builder
Stephens, Fred. Farmer
Toms, Francis, Carpenter
Waldron, Henry, Market Gardener
Webber and Stedham, Brick makers
Woods, H., Victory Inn

Woodland Villa A.F.C., Honicknowle, Season 1913-14

Proudly sat with their trophies for the season are D. C. Arkinson, E. Cowling, E. Doidge, C. Holmes, F. Waldron, S. Nichols, H. Reddings, W. Jasper, G. Colmer, W. Haywood, J. Coombes, N. Foster, A. Snell, W. Mitchell, W. Atwill, captain, P Buchan, W. Groves, E. Fairweather, C. Bravin, D. Holmes, E. Lewis, Captain Wemywss, R. N., President, R. Blackler, S. Thomas, J. Shears and J. Coughlan. The team was in the Devon League and won the cup for this season.

Woodland Villa Y.M.C.A. team about 1920

This under eighteen's team are pictured here in Warwick Park House grounds. Sam Fairweather, Mr. Gray, Mr. Blackler, Mr. F. Male, Mr. W. Packer, Charlie Gray, Edgar Lewis, Sidney Nicholls, Reg. Palmer, Russell Frost, Jasper Bowden, Albert Jasper, Harry Tucker, B. Pengelley, Ron Hodge, Arthur Bravin, Billy Roberts and Bert George make up this fine group of players and supporters.

Woodland Villa, Plymouth and District League, 1920s

The dense vegetation growing on Woodland Fort forms the background to this team photographed sometime in the 1920s. Recognised are Mr. Hobbs (with the walking stick), Mr. F. Mace, Mr. Clift, Bernie Pengelley, Reg. Palmer, Fred Hurrell, Paddy Lock, Albert Jasper, Charlie Gray, Harry Friend, Mr. Blackler, Harry Chowings, George Hobbs, Ron Hobbs, Bill Hodges, Stan Hodge and Dick Mayne.

"VILLAGE FAYRE" AT HONICKNOWLE.

RE-OPENING OF THE RECREATION HALL.

October 1927

A GREAT WORK.

Yesterday afternoon Mrs. Sydney Castle, of Plymouth, reopened the Honicknowle Reading and Recreation Association's hall, which has recently been extended, and gave a send off to the "Village Fayre," which was held in the hall, to augment the funds of the Association.

Performing the opening ceremony, Mrs. Castle said: "I am sure you have all worked very hard, and I think it is a great boon to the young people of the village to have a place like this to come to during the long winter evenings." She explained that her husband, who is vice-president of the Association, was fulfilling an engagement in the North, and that he joined with her in wishing the Association every success.

Mrs. Castle was presented with a beautiful bouquet by little Master Desmond Evans.

A Wonderful Work.

Major P. Kenyon-Slaney, M.P., proposing a vote of thanks to Mrs. Castle, said he was sure they all appreciated the work that had been done in the hall during the last two or three years. "I have been astonished by the wonderful good work you have done here," he remarked. "Without very much money behind you and by co-operative effort you have provided a hall which will, without doubt, improve the family circle of the village life in Honicknowle. Everyone who has worked to establish this building is to be congratulated, not only by us but by those who come after us."

Seconding the vote of thanks, the Rev. R. J. R. Skipper, vicar of St. Budeaux, said that the people of Honicknowle were a keen set of people, and when they put their hands to the plough there was no turning back. With the increased number of houses being erected in the district they needed to have as large a hall as possible. He hoped the young people would make full use of the hall, and that the social gatherings held there from time to time would be for the good of the people morally and spiritually. Mr. E. C. Coffin supported.

Major Kenyon-Slaney's Generosity.

Mr. E. Lewis, the hon. secretary, announced that children over 12 years of age could borrow books on Monday nights free of cost. Making an appeal for funds, Mr. Lewis mentioned that there was a debt of £10 outstanding on the flower show and that they were anxious that enough should be raised to clear the deficit.

Major Kenyon-Slaney had a conversation with the hon. treasurer, Mr. Lee, who immediately consulted Mr. Lewis, and he announced that the Major had promised to lift this financial burden from their shoulders.

The gratitude of the people of Honicknowle for his generosity was conveyed to Major Slaney in tumultuous plaudits and hearty cheering.

The Stallholders.

The stallholders were:—New stall, Messrs. Tucker, Male. Jumble, Messrs. Cook, Ham, Chapman. Pound and vegetables, Messrs. Lee, G. Shears, Doidge, Sharp. Refreshments, Mesdames Fairweather Bishop, May, Blackler, Clift. Dip, Miss D. Lewis. Competition, Mrs. Lewis. Fortune Doll, Miss E. Sharp.

The results of the baby show and fancy dress competitions were:—

Fancy Dress.—1, Marjorie Pollard (Queen of Sheba); 2, Irene Hobbs (Autumn); 3, Lilian Lakeman (Miss Muffet). Boys.—1, Derrick Pollard (Posy of Roses); 2, Thornton Kingshot (Frenchman); 2, Clarence Peard (Dutch Boy); consolation prize, Desmond Evans (Boy Blue).

Baby Show.—Under six months.—Cynthia Stevenson. Under twelve months.—1, Maurice Crago; 2, Cecil Brimacombe; 3, Dennis Newman. Under two years.—1, Mavis Chowings; 2, Baby Mitchell; 3, Edna Atwill. Special.—Local Baby—Cecil Brimacombe. Special—brought up on Neave's Food—Raymond Kingshot.

Boundary and Milestone

The above stone still stands in Little Dock Lane and shows the extension of the old Borough of Devonport in 1898. The lower stone is now missing and shows that the Honicknowle area was five miles from Dock which changed its name to Devonport in 1824. The stone probably dates from the 1700s and some of its letters are missing, probably caused by damage from passing carts.

The First Carnival, 1933

This shot records part of the bunting announcing the coming of Honicknowle Week, 28th August to 2nd September. Butt Park Road is now looking empty but other photographs will show it packed with visitors from all over Plymouth to watch the splendid procession pass along the road. Perhaps the lady with the dog can be recognised?

Boys' Brigade, 1st Honicknowle Company

Members are seen here marching and appealing to save their company which ceased in 1921. It started in 1914 under Captain William Pearce with Lieutenants Edgar Lewis, William Mitchell and James Cole and was connected with the then United Methodist Church. The chaplain was the Rev. Robert Ripley, Devonport. The boys are marching past the *Woodland Fort Inn* presumably sometime during 1921.

Outside the Recreation Hut

This early 1930s picture shows the centre lady holding a decorated horseshoe but for what occasion cannot be recalled. The faces, however, are familiar including that of Mr. F. Male, Mrs. Davies, Mrs. M. Chapman and Mr. Blackler.

Cottage by Boger's Farm

The crossroads of Little Dock Lane and Coombe Park Lane by Boger's Farm then worked by Mr. F. Baker stand close to this old cottage just prior to demolition and new road construction. The old Bickham House is in the far right background.

The Old Chapel

The old Methodist chapel stood in Farm Lane and was used for a variety of meetings after services in it were transferred to the present chapel which opened in 1901. Lantern shows, anniversary teas, Sunday School, under Mr. W. Packer, and the Band of Hope and Boys' Brigade met there. The building became derelict during the war and was demolished during the 1950s.

1935 Queen, Agnes Lewis

A very proud moment is recorded here when Agnes left the decorated house to take up duties during the carnival week. Her maids of honour were Betty Hooper and Hazel Palmer. She was crowned by Mrs. S. B. Stedham and is seen here wearing a white satin dress. The Queen opened the fayre and attended various events during the busy week.

Maypole Dancing

Local children form a circle around the pole for staging one of the many attractions for the 1933 carnival week. Here under the direction of A. Lewis, senior, they gave a display on the closing day of the week much to the delight of their parents and many visitors.

Farmer May

A rural scene was very familiar not all that many years ago. Here Mr. May stands with one of his cows and calf to the right with Agnes Lewis sometime during 1933. The brickwork's chimney was part of the local scene behind the houses at the rear of the field.

PROCESSION DAY AT HONICKNOWLE

1933

Village's Achievement

LIVE FOX CARRIED BY "HUNTSMAN"

"Honicknowle Week" procession exceeded the organizers' most sanguine hopes last night, and was a remarkable achievement for such a small community.

The Soprani Novelty Band, under the direction of Mr. A. Adams, in their attractive Argentine costumes, led the way, followed by the "Queen" of Honicknowle (Miss Hilda Pearn) and her attendants, Misses Ina Male and Constance Brimacombe.

Then came decorated wagons full of laughing children in fancy dress, and a large number of adults, some in fancy dress, and others wearing grotesque masques and heads.

The Oddfellows sent two tableaux on motor lorries, and the Plymouth Co-operative Society, the London Furnishing Co., and the Western Counties Brick Co., Ltd., were also represented. The latter firm's entry was particularly interesting. Mr. William Sharp, of South Down, Millbrook, demonstrating the art of making bricks by hand.

HAND-MADE BRICKS.

Mr. Sharp, who is employed by the Western Counties Brick Co., has been making hand-made bricks for 60 years. He is believed to be the only man in the district who can now make bricks by this method, which has been superseded by machinery.

Mr. J. Rowe entered two of his cream-coloured donkeys. He has kept donkeys in Honicknowle for over forty years. On one of the animals was Master Lee, dressed as the Honicknowle town crier.

Mr. W. Davies, dressed as a huntsman, came next, riding a black pony and carrying a live fox, aged five months.

Tossing the Coin

The traditional way on deciding on which team plays in what direction is recorded here at the start of the Saturday afternoon football match. Two gallant teams of local ladies don shirts and shorts for this part of the 1933 carnival week in the field just below the Methodist Chapel seen in the background. Evelyn Bishop and Agnes Lewis look skywards expectantly.

1933 Queen, Hilda Pearn

Part of her many duties during the carnival week was to support the various events including the line up for the local ladies football teams here grouped in front of the goal posts. Doris Tudor scored the two winning goals for the *Black and Green* team who pitted their skill against the *Red and Green* team. Everyone thoroughly enjoyed themselves urged on by many supporters from the village.

HONICKNOWLE DRESS PARADE

1934

Mannequins Make Village History

DISPLAY OF AUTUMN FASHIONS

Carnival "Queen" To View Domain By Air.

HISTORY was made at Honicknowle yesterday, the fifth day of the village carnival week, when an attractive mannequin parade was held in the hall of the Reading and Recreation Association, in aid of which the carnival has been organized.

The building was recently extended at a cost of nearly £300, and it is hoped that the proceeds of the carnival will assist materially in defraying the cost. The residents of Honicknowle and many visitors from Plymouth have rallied round the committee in an attempt to make the Week a much greater success than last year.

Yesterday's event was the first mannequin parade ever held at Honicknowle, and the hall was crowded with women eager to see the new autumn fashions.

The parade was carried out by Messrs. Costers, Ltd., Plymouth, and there were eight mannequins.

The platform was attractively decorated, with a large white horseshoe as the centrepiece. Electric lights formed the greeting "Success to your Week." The arrangements were carried out by Mr. Geoffrey Leatherby, with Miss Betty Griffiths as the announcer.

A Young Entrant

Children's competitions, fancy dress shows and sports featured in most of the 1930 carnivals. This youngster has not been recognised but he is the centre of attraction for the bystanders and is here hopefully waiting for his turn to move in the hope of gaining a prize for himself and the decorated hand cart.

Queen with Ladies Football Team, 1934

Eileen Stevens is here wishing the captain good luck for the match which was watched by about 2,000 people according to newspaper reports. Mr. A. E. Doidge was the referee for this fifteen minute each way game on a half size pitch. The shirts were borrowed from local clubs.

Oh! to be Young Again

A not unfamiliar wish for many adults but few would dare to dress up like this with a dummy in expectation of a prize. Adults certainly joined in the fun of the carnival although these here have not been named. Do you know them?

Local Horse and Cart

A bowler-hatted Reg. Bennetto is dressed for this carnival entry in the early 1930s. He worked as a farm labourer for Mr. May whose horse and cart added to the country atmosphere of the annual carnival. The horse and cart looked suitably cleaned and ready at the start for the parade and judges.

A Pair of Horses

Dick Lowden, who worked for Freddie Baker, the farmer, stands with George Spencer waiting for the start of the parade in Butt Park Road. The second horse dressed as the first looks like a team entry for the occasion.

Children up High

A very good position to be for the carnival procession thought to be driven by Reg. Bennetto. One girl has been recognised as Agnes Lewis. Part of the word "Honicknowle" is on the front of the waggon.

Maypole Dancers Entry Group
Grandpa Lewis sits with the various dancers on this cart entered for the 1934 carnival. He is at the back with a beard and hat obviously enjoying himself with the youngsters. Among these are Constance Brimacombe, Winnie and Lily Lee, Beryl Ivey, Millie Shears, Joyce Chapman and Mary McKee. It shows the group in Butt Park Road on the special year of the hut's extension.

A Bicycle made for One!
The year is 1935 and Agnes Lewis proudly stands with what looks like a new bike. There was certainly no traffic about in those days and Woodland Fort was then used as a home for various families occupying some of its rooms.

Outside the Chapel
Although some of the people have been recognised the occasion for them coming together cannot be recalled. Is Sam Fairweather holding a Bible? Does this give a clue to the occasion? Edgar Lewis is on the left and Eddie Evans, Mr. Blackler (he gave cart rides to local children), Mr. and Mrs. Gill and Mrs. Titmus have been recognised.

Farm Horses on Parade

Uncle Tom Cobleigh and All was the entry for this group in the 1934 village carnival. George Spencer is here with many of the local horses which worked the land of the various Honicknowle farms. The support for the carnival came from all around and from out of Plymouth. This parade shows clearly the interest local people had in the land.

The Policeman's House

P.C. Friendship, P.C. Fred Barry and P.C. Radford names should bring back memories to many youngsters of the village. Here the Devon Constabulary house is decorated for one of the carnivals in which the local bobby took an active part.

A New Queen is Crowned, 1934

Florence Ivey, the carnival Queen for 1934, is here receiving the crown from Hilda Pearn her predecessor in 1933. The new attendants are Mahala Cronshaw and Lilian Lakeman suitably dressed with head decorations for the occasion. Neighbours and friends gathered to watch this event for the start of the Honicknowle week.

Dressed for the Extension

The long and much beloved "rec" hut is here decked with bunting and covered with new paint to celebrate its extensive use and extension. The year was 1934 and many hundreds of people have used the hut since.

Honicknowle Reading and Recreation Association.

Re-Opening Recreation Hall

AFTER EXTENSION

SATURDAY, AUGUST 18th, 1934

at 3 p.m. by

MR. MARK PATRICK, M.P.

7 p.m.— CONCERT

by Miss Geraldine Lamb's Pupils.

Selection of Miss Honicknowle and Attendants during the interval. (Entries close August 16th)

Admission 6d.   Children 2d.

"HONICKNOWLE WEEK" AUGUST 26th to SEPT. 1st

Buy a Souvenir Programme, 2d., and win a handsome clock.

Further Details E. H. T. Lewis, Hon. Organising Secretary, Tremarys, Honicknowle.

Dingle & Co., Printers, St. Budeaux.

HONICKNOWLE
READING & RECREATION ASSOCIATION

Tenth Annual Exhibition
POULTRY, PIGEONS & RABBITS

RECREATION ROOM, HONICKNOWLE,
On Saturday, December 21st, 1935.

Recreation Hall Extensions, 1934

Due to growing demands on the general use of the hall it was extended in 1934 (see notice above) and was re-opened by Mr. Mark Patrick, M.P. supported by those shown in the accompanying photograph. Mr. F. Male, Mr. A. Sherrill, Mr. E. Ewans, Mr. A. Lee, treasurer, Mr. E. Lewis and Mr. W. Peters have been recognised together with Jean Langworth, the girl holding the flowers. The chairman was Mr. E. Evans. The Reading and Recreation Association made the first improvements to the hut which was first erected by the chapel in 1912 and then moved to the present site in 1925.

Juvenile Sunbeams

A thriving band of youngsters organised by Mr. Edgar Lewis mainly during the late 1920s and early 1930s gave many concerts at Honicknowle and at other places around Plymouth. Here dressed for a performance are May Huck, Lily Tudor, Betty Martin, Mary Windsor, Mahala Crownshaw, Beryl Ivey, Iris Jones and others.

Honicknowle 'Panto'

Mr. E. H. T. Lewis, well known in Honicknowle for his work in connection with charity, last night produced a pantomime at Honicknowle Recreation Hall, proceeds of which were devoted to peace celebrations in connection with Honicknowle Recreation Association.

The story chosen was "Dick Whittington," with Miss Mary Potts as Dick, Miss Thelma Maybourne as Alice, and Marina Arthurs as the Cat. Dancing was provided by pupils of Miss P. Bryant. Music by Mesdames Rapson and Kerslake.

HONICKNOWLE CONCERT

Honicknowle Juvenile Sunbeams gave a concert in the Recreation Room, Honicknowle, last night, comprising songs with illustrations, sketches, and the fairy play "The Flag," to the accompaniment of Mrs. F. Male.

The children were coached by Mr. E. T. H. Lewis.

In an entertainment at Bere Ferrers in aid of Prisoners of War Fund, parts were successfully played by the Woodland Stars Dancing Troupe of Honicknowle, Miss Mildred Lyle (pianist), Little Jimmy Wakeham (soprano), Messrs. John Ferrand and E. L. Lewis.

Honicknowle Juvenile Concert Party

These were organised by Mr. Lewis before the carnivals of the 1930s. For three years from 1925 performances were staged at the then "Devon Mental Hospital, Exminster" (near Exeter) in which Marjory Miller, Irene Gibbons, Agnes Lewis, John Male, Miss B. Evans, E. Banfield, D. Atwill, D. Lewis and G. May gave an interesting range of entertainment. The pianist was Mrs. Male.

A Local Show

Mr. and Mrs. E. Lewis stand with their group of young artists for another show in the recreation hut. The year has not been given but it looks around the early 1930s. Joan Ellery, Joyce Chapman and Flo Leighton have been identified and the houses at the back will be familiar to local residents at Honicknowle.

Honicknowle. 1937

- Allen H. May View house
- Atwill W, Stewart cotts
- Avery W. F. 5 Fort cotts
- Baker F. Honicknowle farm
- Banfield J. 16 Butt pk terr
- Baskerville J. 3 Woodland Fort cotts
- Blackler R T, Mount Pleasant
- Beavel W J, Mt. Plesant
- Bolton Mrs. 6 Woodland Park cotts
- Bowden E. Alexandra cotts
- Bowden J. 25 Butt park terr
- Bowden Mrs. 2 Primrose cots
- Brown H E, 1 Glendale
- Burn T. 1a Butt pk terr
- Burnam J, 2 Glendale cotts
- Callaway J. 5 Fort cots
- Cholwill A, 1 Alexandra cots
- Chowing H, 8 Horsham cotts
- Cole J. 11 Butt park terr
- Cole W, 17 Butt park terr genl dealer
- Cole W. J, 15 Butt park terr
- Collins W. 2 Stroud cots
- Colmar R, 5 Primrose cotts
- Connolly J E, Woodland Fort Inn
- Cook H E. 14 Horsham cotts
- Corry J, 11 Quarry cotts
- Coughlan J, 39 Butt pk terr
- Cowling Mrs. 4 Fort cotts
- Cudlip F, 1 Horsham cotts
- Dawe J, 32 Butt park terr
- Dawson J, 'Victory inn'
- Dunster W. J. 7 Horsham cot
- Edgecumbe F. Stuart cotts
- Evans Edwin, Mount Pleasant
- Evans Mrs E, 24 Butt park terr
- Fairweather W, 36 Butt pk terr
- Finnemore R, 7 Fort cotts
- Fone G. 3 Glendale cotts
- Foulkes R. 2 Horsham cotts
- Friend H. 1 Primrose cots
- Gammon — 10 Quarry cotts
- Gray G. 21 Butt park terr
- Gray J. 12 Butt park terr
- Gray S, 22 Butt park terr
- Grey J, 2 Rose cotts
- Grey Mrs, 10 Horsham cotts
- Harris W, 9 Quarry cott
- Haywood E. J. 33 Butt park terr
- Heard R, 28 Butt park terr
- Herod F R, 7 Butt pk terr
- Hill G. 2 Primrose cot
- Hockings J, 6 Butt park terr
- Hodder H. 5 Woodland Fort cotts
- Hodge W, 26 Butt park terr
- Holmes Mrs A. 8 Butt park terr
- Hortop J F, Bush vll
- Hoskin K, 34 Butt park terr
- Hoskin W. H. 4 Fort cots
- Hosswell J. W. Burnton farm
- Hullam W. C. H. Stuart cotts
- Hurst C senr. 14 Butt park terr
- Hurst C, 10 Butt park terr
- Hutchings J, May cott
- Hutchings P. C. 31 Butt Pk ter
- Jasper R, Watts cott
- Jenkins Mrs. 3 Quarry cotts
- Kingwell G, 7 Butt park terr
- Kingwell W. J. 9 Butt pk terr
- Lang T, Victory cotts
- Langworthy G, Bogers farm
- Lavers G. H. 6 Primrose cots
- Lay G. Round House
- Lewis A, 18 Butt park terr
- Long R. M. 5 Horsham pl
- Maddock W. 1 Strouds cots
- Matthews Mrs, Mount Pleasant
- Maunder J, 3 Rose cotts
- May W, Stewart cotts
- May W, Stewart pl
- McKay W, 3 Alexandra cotts
- Mitchell J. 29 Butt park terr
- Mortimore E T. Alexandra cot
- Moyon C. 4 Fort cotts
- Nicholls Mrs, 9 Horsham cotts
- Oliver Mrs. 19 & 20 Butt pk ter draper & P.O.
- Palmer T, 85 Butt pk terr
- Peard Mrs, 30 Butt park terr
- Pearn C. N. 27 Butt park terr
- Pengelly J, 13 Butt park terr genl dealer
- Pengelly Mrs. J. 1 Rose cotts
- Pengelly Mrs, 4 Alexandra cotts
- Petherbridge H. 2 Woodland Fort cots
- Pitt C. Butt park terr
- Pollard W. 38 Butt pk terr
- Reading B, 8 Alexandra cotts
- Rendell J, Bush vll
- Rice F, 6 Quarry cotts
- Roberts F. 2 Butt Pk terr
- Rodgers J, 4 Butt park terr
- Rowe J, 37 Butt park terr
- Rowe J, Watts cott
- Sacre W. 3 Glendale cots
- Scott Elliott Capt. A.S.C. Warwick Park
- Seldon G. T. 3 Butt park terr
- Seldon W, 1 Woodland Fort cotts
- Sharman G. 1 Quarry cotts
- Shazell A, Mt. Plesant
- Shears T. 3 Horsham cots
- Shears W, 6 Fort cotts
- Shears R, 6 Alexandra cotts
- Shears S, 12 Horsham cotts
- Smith R. 8 Quarry cots
- Smith W C, F, Bickham pk hse
- Spencer Mrs, Round House
- Spencer Mrs. Bogers cotts
- Stevens G, Bush vll
- Stevens Mrs M, 4 Horsham cotts
- The Brick Co. Crownhill
- Thorne G, 4 Quarry cotts
- Thorne G A, 2 Quarry cotts
- Thorne W. 7 Quarry cotts
- Toms F, 1 Primrose cots
- Trice Mrs. 5 Butt park ter
- Trust H E, 23 Butt park terr
- Tucker H. Mount Pleasant
- United Methodist Church
- Vaughan A. G. 3 Stewart cots
- Waldron H, The Tenement farm
- Wallis G. 4 Primrose cots
- Walters J, 6 Horsham cotts
- Ware, H., 4 Glendale cotts
- Welch T H, 3 Primrose cots
- Williams G, 4 Alexandra cots
- Williams J, 5 Quarry cotts
- Willcocks Mrs. 6 Fort cots
- Worth J. 7 Fort cotts
- Wilson G. 1 Woodland Fort cots
- Wonnicott G. 13 Horsham cot

Honicknowle Reading & Recreation Association

HONICKNOWLE WEEK, 1939

EDGAR H. T. LEWIS, Hon. Organiser.

OFFICIALS.

President	S. B. STEDHAM, Esq.
Chairman	E. EVANS, Esq.
Vice-Chairman	C. HURST, Esq.
Hon. Treasurer	C. HURST, Esq.

Committee :
MESSRS. J. SHARP, R. WILLIAMS, F. MALE, W. CHAPMAN, W. FIELDING, H. FRIEND, C. SHARP, C. SHEARS, W. BEER, HONICKNOWLE READING AND RECREATION ASSN. COMMITTEE ASSISTED BY FRIENDS.

HONICKNOWLE

Honicknowle, about one mile east-south-east from the ancient and historical Parish Church of St. Budeaux, derives its name from one of the five manors in the Parish of St. Budeaux, became part of the added area to the City of Plymouth on the 1st April this year.

DEAR FRIENDS,
The gratifying results of last year, for which we thank you, enabled the Committee to have the building railed off. It gives us every encouragement to look forward to our Seventh great Week, we trust with the result to improve the interior of the Hall.
We have endeavoured to provide for your entertainment. This would not be possible if it were not for the many willing helpers and friends who give their time and service to make the Week a success, for which I record the Committee's and my personal appreciation. May the carnival spirit enter this effort, and may every one, without exception, enjoy every item shown in this Programme.
EDGAR H. T. LEWIS, Hon. Organiser.
"Tremarys," Honicknowle, Plymouth.

YOUTHFUL RIVALS AT HONICKNOWLE

1939

170 Baby Show Entries

"QUEEN" SPECTATOR AT JUDGING

There were 170 entries for the baby show, one of the main features of Honicknowle Week, which continued yesterday.
Of this number 150 were entered for the open classes, and 20 in the local class.
Interested spectators in the Recreation Hall, which was crowded with mothers and babies, were the "Queen" (Miss J. Chapman) and her Attendants, Misses M. Fox and I. Walling.
A boxing exhibition was well attended during the evening, but owing to the inclement weather the alfresco dance in the street was cancelled.

ALL-IN WRESTLING.

Clever bouts were given by Gnr. Dunn and Gnr. Darlington, Gnr. Hooper and Gnr. Stitson, Lce.-Bdmr. Hearn and Gnr. Scallan, Gnr. Storey and Flash Acton, Gnr. Doel and Joe Fletcher, Gnr. Horsham and Gnr. Todd.
Mr. H. Farrall, a member of the British Boxing Board of Control, acted as referee, in place of Mr. F. Ash (ex-contender for the world's title), who has been called up. Mr. F. J. Male was M.C. and Mr. R. Vinnicombe timekeeper.

UNBEATEN RECORD MAINTAINED

"Amazons" In Honicknowle Football Match

1937

HOME TEAM WIN

Having already beaten Turnchapel and Hooe and Plympton this season, Honicknowle Ladies A.F.C. gained another victory on their home ground against the former last evening by three goals to one.
The occasion was the second day of Honicknowle Week.
Although the visiting team arrived an hour late, spectators kept filing into the ground, and when the game began there were just over 1,000 people present, including supporters from Turnchapel and Hooe, who had arrived by char-à-banc.
Both teams were presented to "Miss Honicknowle" (Miss Eileen Stevens), who kicked off.
The home side proved the better throughout, and led by two goals, both scored by Joan Ellery, at the interval.
On the resumption Honicknowle went further ahead with a goal from Kathleen Jones, but the visitors fought gamely and were rewarded with a goal by Joan Smith.

VISITORS BRING MASCOT.

Throughout the game the crowd were amused by some "fooling" from the visitors' mascot, Mrs. Tucker, aged 60.
She was even allowed, half-way through the first half, to dribble the ball to the Honicknowle goal, but even then her shot hit the post.
Speaking to a "Western Morning News" representative, Miss F. Leighton, captain of Honicknowle, said they first played as a team two years ago, and last year they had been unbeaten.
"This year," she said, "we have already beaten Turnchapel 2—1 and Plympton 4—2, so now it only remains for us to beat Plympton on Saturday and we shall again be unbeaten.
"After playing Plympton on Saturday we shall pack up for the season, unless we have a challenge from any other team,' she added.

Following the boxing, two local lads, "Popeye" Davis and "Killer" Walling gave an exhibition of all-in wrestling. There was also a bout between Jerry Hanley and Don Luxton.
The "Queen" and her Attendants were present, and music was played by the C. S. Orchestra.

BABY SHOW AWARDS.

Up to 6 months— 1, Jean Spencer; 2, Ronald Lawes; 3, Terence Williams. 6 to 12 months—1, Patricia Windle; 2, David John Williams; 3, Frank Moore. 1 year to 1½ years—1, Peter Bennett; 2, Wendy Petre Nepean; 3, Roger Willcocks. 1½ years to 2 years—1, Derek Alfred George Hould; 2, Carole Ann Perver; 3, Jean Ruby Rochester.
Twins, up to 2 years—1, Stephen Philpott and Sidney Philpott; 2, Mavis Evans and Mary Evans. Local class—Valerie Tate.
The Millbay Laundry Cup for the best baby in the show was won by Peter Bennett, aged one year.
Dr. F. Fox, Miss E. Hyslop and Miss O. Johns were the judges.

FURRY DANCE AT HONICKNOWLE

1938

Last Night's Success

JUVENILE TALENT COMPETITION

Last night's Furry Dance was the outstanding feature of yesterday's festivities in connection with Honicknowle Carnival Week.

In the morning "Miss Honicknowle" (Miss Peggy McKee), with her Attendants, visited the old people and the sick in the district. They also went to West Park, which is just inside the Plymouth boundary, and later distributed prize-money for the best decorated houses.

The Juvenile Talent competition was held in the village hall in the afternoon, when the singing, dancing, and other items were of a high standard. A somewhat original turn was that given by Miss Iris Jones (Honicknowle), who delighted a large audience with self-taught acrobatic feats, which, for a child, were remarkable. Miss Molly Banks gave an admirable rendering of "It's better to have loved and lost." Results: 1, and cup. Miss B. Rattenbury (St. Budeaux); 2, and gold and silver medal, Miss K. Powton (Stoke); 3, and silver medal, Master T. Hender (Stoke).

Judges were: Mr A C Cann and Mesdames R. Annear and Robbins. Entries totalled 45

TRUE CORNISH STYLE.

The band of the Saltash Working Men's Club led Furry Dancers through the streets to the tune of the "Helston Floral Dance." A troupe of girl dancers at the head of the procession entered a number of houses in true Cornish style. Much amusement was caused when the troupe danced into an orchard and came out eating apples and pears. Dancing went on for nearly two hours.

The revels ended with a cabaret ball in the hall. The C.S. Orchestra was in attendance and features were the performances of the Can Can and Hawaiian dancers. Later dancing continued in the main street, music being relayed from the hall. Mr. A Collins was M.C.

FREE FLIGHT WINNER.

The winner of the draw for a free flight with "Miss Honicknowle" and her Attendants today is Mr. A. W. Henby, of 48, Portland-road, Stoke. A 'plane will leave Plymouth Airport at 4.30 and cruise over Honicknowle.

1938 Queen with Attendants

The three splendid girls pose for the photographer with Edgar Lewis on the left. Peggy McKee was the Queen for this year and her maids of honour were Christine Pook and Gladys Cashmore.

Furry Dance

Details of this occasion in 1938 are recorded here in this newspaper article and the photograph below shows one of the many houses open to the jubilant dancers making their way from home to home.

Outside the Recreation Hut, 1939

This was the last occasion for nine years that the village engaged in the popular Honicknowle week. Joyce Chapman is the Queen and poses with Iris Walling and Myra Fox, her two maids of honour, for the privilege of leading the many events of the annual week at the end of August and start of September.

1943 Christmas Party

200 children attended the thirtieth annual party held in the recreation hut on Saturday, 2nd January, 1943. Father Christmas is H. S. Thomas, seen here with children, and Edgar Lewis. There was a Charlie Chaplin film, tea and games organised by J. Davies and R. Huck with Mrs. R. Kerslake at the piano. H. Prince, R. Williams, H. Thomas and Mesdames E. Lewis, J. Sharp, C. Hurst and J. Beer also assisted with this well enjoyed event.

Kick Off for the 1945 Season

Football has always had a strong following in the village. Since 1900 various teams have had many successes in the different leagues and three of these are featured in these pages. No names have come forward for the occasion shown here but the elderly man still stoutly kicks the ball at some point during the first season after the war.

31st Annual Party at the "Rec"

This group photograph shows the New Year's Party in full swing at the recreation hut in January, 1944. Some two hundred and fifty children were feasted and entertained seen here with helpers under the direction of Mr. Edgar Lewis. No doubt many of today's adults will recognise themselves as children in those now distant war days.

HONICKNOWLE CARNIVAL SPIRIT
1948

Great Interest In Revived Event

Honicknowle's carnival, the first since 1939, which opened last night, is attracting more attention than ever before, chiefly because of the growth of the housing estates in the district.

The recreation hall, where the send-off took place, had never held so many people. The proceedings were relayed to crowds of people in the street. They heard the Deputy Lord Mayor of Plymouth (Ald. L. J. Hodge), who opened the carnival, congratulate the hard-working committee.

And when the speeches were finished they were heard again. Arranged by Mr. H. L. Trebilcock, city councillor, everything was recorded and played back.

DANCING IN STREET

Miss Meril Stentiford, the Carnival Queen, was crowned by Mrs. H. D. Gill, who was presented with a bouquet by Miss P. Williams. The two Attendants were presented with bouquets by Miss J. Boswell.

In 1939, 19-years-old Joyce Chapman was "Miss Honicknowle." Now she is Mrs. J. Buzz, lives in Birkenhead, and is the mother of a child. But she is down for the carnival, and last night presented a bouquet to the "Queen."

Following a concert by the Magpies, there was dancing in the street until 11.0, as there will be every night this week.

Honicknowle Recreation Association.

President : Group Captain C. L. Pendlebury.
Chairman : Mr. E. H. T. Lewis.
Vice-Chairman : Mr. C. Hurst.
Hon. Treasurer : Mr. A. Lee.
Carnival Committee: Messrs. Chapman, Prince, Friend, Jury, Williams, Slater, Bishop, Kelly, R. Lee.
Mesdames Lewis, Hurst, Chapman, Prince, Williams, Jury, Lee, Slater, Hurst, senr., Davies, Palmer, Summers, Shears.

Dear Friends,
The gratifying results of last year, for which we thank you, enabled the Committee to assist fifteen charities.
This year the proceeds will be devoted towards the cost of painting the Hall and fifty per cent. to charity.
May the Carnival Spirit enter this effort, and every item shown in the programme be enjoyed.
Arrangement will be made for "Miss Honicknowle" to visit anybody at their homes in the neighbourhood, if through infirmity or sickness, they are unable to attend the Carnival.

EDGAR H. T. LEWIS,
Hon. Organiser,
57 Crownhill Road, Plymouth.

SUNDAY, AUGUST 27th.
OPEN-AIR RELIGIOUS SERVICE, at 3.0 p.m.
Conducted by the Rev. F. H. SUTTON.
Address by MAJOR A. MILLS (Salvation Army).
Singing led by the SHAFTESBURY SALVATION ARMY BAND.

7.45 p.m.—C O N C E R T by
THE "BERKERTEX" CHOIR
(Conducted by Mrs. M. E. BARBARY).
Admission : Adults, 6d. ; Children, 3d.

MONDAY, AUGUST 28th, 7.0 p.m.

Official Opening and Crowning Ceremony
BY
MRS. LUCY MIDDLETON, M.P.

THE PEDLAR BROTHERS
of
Carrol Levis and B.B.C. Fame
present an
ALL STAR VARIETY SHOW.
Admission : Adults, 2/- ; Children, 1/-.
Prizes will be awarded for Decorated Houses or Business Premises in Woodland Villas and Butt Park Road.

10 to 11.0 p.m.—ALFRESCO DANCE IN THE STREET.

Big parade at Honicknowle Carnival
1949

WAGONS, HORSES DECORATED

THE highlight of the fourth stage of Honicknowle Carnival Week was a procession of decorated wagons and horses last evening.

Thirteen Carnival Queens from other districts of Plymouth, and from neighbouring towns, were among the people who took part in the procession, which was the largest in the history of the carnival.

The 130 entrants in the fancy dress competition also paraded. The first prize winners in this event were Valerie Steele, Joy Nicholas, D. Gosling, and Jill Anniss.

JUVENILE TALENT

"Miss Honicknowle" (Miss Joan Slater) presented the prizes to the winners of the juvenile talent competition, which took place in the afternoon.

The judges said that the standard of the entries was high, and it was difficult to decide upon the winners.

The prizewinners were: Under 10—1, Wendy Hird; 2, Jennifer Trout; 3, Freda Becken. Under 15—1, Ernest Carwithen; 2, Pauline Hunt; 3, Thelma Gosley.

The day ended with an old 'time dance and an alfresco dance in the street.

A Smiling Queen

Joan Slater, the Queen for 1949, is smiling with her attendants Shirley Street and Muriel Nicholson. It looks like they are in a car in procession through the village.

Honicknowle Air View For *1948* Carnival Queen

FORMATION FLIGHT OVER PLYMOUTH

In brilliant sunshine the first post-war Carnival Week at Honicknowle ended on Saturday with this year's "Queen" viewing her "domain" from the air.

In the leading aircraft of three, which flew over Plymouth in formation, "Miss Honicknowle," 17-years-old Meril Stentiford, made her first flight ever. She was accompanied by her two Attendants, also flying for the first time.

"Miss Honicknowle" at the 1939 carnival, the last to be held, Mrs. J. Buzz (now of Birkenhead) and one of her Attendants flew in a second aircraft, and two officials were in the third.

The seat reserved for the winner of the free air cruise was not taken. He did not appear at take-off time.

Result of a children's fancy dress competition: 1, Jessie Huck; 2, Barbara Taylor; 3, Pat Trevey. Most original dress—1, Susan Pratt; 2, Maureen Trevey; 3, John Clark. Decorated vehicle—Margaret Batten.

Queen takes to the Air

Three planes flew in formation over Plymouth as part of the carnival celebrations, the first carrying Meril Stentiford, the Queen, and her two attendants. The second carried the 1939 Queen, who came down specially from Birkenhead for the event, and the last held two officials. The full group are here at Plymouth airport ready for their flights.

Freedom of the Guild

The six ladies proudly hold their certificates giving them the Freedom of the Guild after twenty-one years' service. There are Mrs. V. Doidge, Mrs. Atwill, Mrs. A. Lang, Mrs. M. Chapman, Mrs. Leighton and Mrs. A. Bartlett. The Co-operative Guild was formed fifty-three years ago and still meets each week in Woodland Fort. It has been very well supported over the years and is enjoyed by a great many local people.

Fortieth Anniversary of the Co-operative Guild at Honicknowle

Mrs. G. Palmer wearing the president's chain of office for this occasion stands with Mr. Moore from the Plymouth Co-operative Society and friends at Woodland Fort. Mrs. M. Vincent, Mrs. P. Bowley, Mrs. Hodges, Mrs. Gregory, Mrs. H. Hodges, Mrs. Sponheimer, Mrs. K. Babb, Mrs. Whitehouse, Mrs. Elliott, Mrs. E. Palmer, Mrs. A. Worth, Mrs. Doidge, Mrs. F. Cholwill and Mrs. Kirk make up part of this smiling group of members.

Fourth Birthday Party, 1959

All smiles and good food in the recreation hut reflect this occasion when 130 members of the National Federation of Old Age Pensioners came together for their fourth birthday party at Honicknowle. It took place on 13th January and the chief guest was the Lord Mayor of Plymouth, Alderman G. J. Wingett and the Lady Mayoress. Table flowers were by Mrs. Clegg and her daughter Mrs. P. Peree.

1950 Carnival Queen

Valetta Pope is being crowned Honicknowle's Carnival Queen by Mrs. Lucy Middleton, M.P., watched by her attendants Sheila Welch and Muriel Nicholson. Also in the happy group are Group Captain C. L. Pendlebury, president, and Edgar H. T. Lewis, the carnival chairman. The ceremony took place in the recreation hut and it was reported that for the first time there would not be a fair linked with the carnival week.

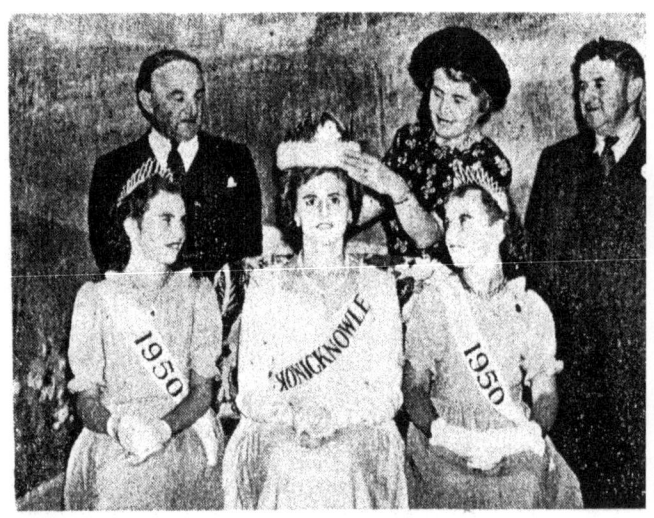

Visit of the Mayor in 1950

Mr. E. Lewis casts a careful eye over the Mayor, Alderman Mrs. J. Marshall, and a child pulling a cracker during the Christmas party held at Honicknowle. A well supported event was enjoyed by all including the various adult helpers.

Paper Hats and Smiles

These give a clue to the occasion which was one of many in celebration of the Queen's coronation in 1952. It was taken in 77 Butt Park Road showing Mr. and Mrs. F. Hayman, Mr. and Mrs. Thomas, Mrs. and Miss Tozer with Mr. and Mrs. Palmer in the group and others.

Decorated House

This has not been identified or the lady looking upwards outside of it. The occasion was the coronation in 1952 and aptly shows the style of many houses dressed for this national event.

Woodland Fort Art Class in 1952

Woodland Fort was used during the 1950s for a variety of art and craft classes attended by many local children under the enthusiastic leadership of many adults, one being Mr. Robert Huck seen here at the back. They were on a voluntary basis and covered sculpture, weaving, craft work, etc. The gala week was a focal point at this period for those involved in the Woodland Fort activities. Here the art class is being made up of local children among whom are Jessie Huck, Peter Peree and Jean Oxenham.

Honicknowle Brickworks

These were started in the late 1800s by Webber and Stedham, then by Mr. S. B. Stedham and finally by the Western Counties Brick Company. It closed in 1966 having exhausted much of the clay and more modern techniques were being introduced by the company at Steer Point. One yard was in Butt Park Road and the other was in the old Honicknowle Quarry. both equipped with kilns.

The clay was originally extracted by pick and shovel then with a 19RB excavator with blasting to loosen the ground. Jubilee trucks took it to the grinding mill reducing it to dust with water being added. It passed through a screened feeding floor then into moulds before being put into the brick press. A crown barrow was used to take the bricks to the kilns where they were stacked and fired. Some 18,000 could be produced in a normal nine hour day and these were either delivered by the company's steam waggon or later four lorries, or collected by builders. Facing and building bricks were the bulk of the work's output.

John Sharp, Foreman

He was one of four generations of this family who worked in brickmaking, he himself working at Honicknowle for thirty-seven years, the foreman in charge of the plant. The conveyor from the top to the lower yard can be seen in the lower picture.

Brickwork's Outing, 1932

All set for the work's outing to Cheddar for which each man got 10/- from Mr. Stedham. Jock Summers, Len Hook, Rupert Curry, Harry Chowings, Ernie Whitehead, Bill Grieves, Bill Palmer, Alfie Bridges and Bert Cardy have been recognised.

Honicknowle Farm Cottages

These stood just below the junction of Little Dock Lane with Coombe Park Lane and were the homes of the Jasper and Rowe families at one time. Mr. Rowe was a market gardener. Here they stand empty waiting to make way for the new developments which completely changed Honicknowle from the 1950s. The land around was purchased by the city council for housing and shops, etc.

Old Road Junction

The road to the right leads to Mount Pleasant starting in front of Boger's Farm while the lower road dips past these cottages, the round house just beyond and then to New Farm dairy towards Warwick Park House and the chapel. Bush Villa is just out of the photograph to the left once the home of Mr. J. Rendell.

Little Dock Lane

This early 1950's view across what was once some of Honicknowle's fields has the warning sign "Danger Slow, Men at Work" in the foreground with the brickwork's chimney in the background. Clearance work was just in hand when Mr. N. J. Smith took this shot. A private car and houses in the centre background can also be seen.

Boger's Farm

Many people will recall the days when Honicknowle was surrounded by fields with once familiar farms working the land. This is the old Boger's farmstead last used by Langworthy family of two generations. Mr. G. Langworthy was there followed by his son, Mr. H. Langworthy, with his daughter, Jean. He used horse and carts, had cows and grew corn and root vegetables. It stood at the junction with Farm Lane opposite Bush Villa and a short distance from the original chapel.

Bickham House

A three-wheeled delivery van is making its way up from Weston Mill to serve the people of the then scattered village of Honicknowle surrounded by fields. This 1950's view shows some work on road widening with the house on the left and the old Honicknowle farm on the right.

Little Dock and Honicknowle Lane

This view shows the far side of Bickham House to that shown on the right. The house is partly demolished and was the home of Mr. W. C. F. Smith and his family. Honicknowle farm cottages are on the left, once the home of the Rowes and the Jaspers.

Road at Mount Pleasant

The man walking steadily up past Mount Pleasant and the *Victory Inn*, to the right, has not been recognised nor probably the fields seen here by the people who have moved into the locality since the 1950s. They are now covered by the Chaucer Way and Shakespeare Road houses.

Honicknowle's Bridge

The two private houses in the foreground face each other on the village side of the small bridge which carried the then main road towards Peverell to the right of this view. The photograph is one of the 1950 series showing the back of the *Victory Inn* to the left, the lane leading to Quarry Cottages and the chapel and Warwick Park House in the far background.

Arthur L. Clamp – the man behind the books

Arthur Leslie Clamp was a man of boundless energy with a passion for helping others, particularly through his love of history. A printer by trade, he started his career in a printing company before moving his family from Exeter to Plymouth to teach at the Plymouth College of Art and Design, where he eventually became the Head of the Printing Department.

Arthur with his five children.

A Devoted Family Man

Despite his love of teaching, Arthur prioritised his family, always making it home by 5:30pm for tea. He and his wife, Rosemary, raised five children: Susan, Angela, Elizabeth, David, and Steven. Arthur would often combine his love of family and history by taking his children on Sunday walks, encouraging them to appreciate historical monuments by taking photos or making crayon rubbings of gravestones for his books. The family home at 203 Elburton Road was a hub of activity, with a large garden, featuring a two-storey fort and a makeshift swimming pool.

A Lifelong Learner and Adventurer

Arthur's thirst for knowledge extended beyond history to a deep curiosity about the world. He was passionate about exploring different cultures, traditions, and cuisines, often taking advantage of his long summer holidays as a teacher to travel to places like India, Russia, South America, the middle east and the USA, sometimes bringing one of his children along. This adventurous spirit even influenced his home life, as seen by the short-lived family tradition of steam-cooking vegetables after a trip to Iceland.

History is a prominent feature of family days out

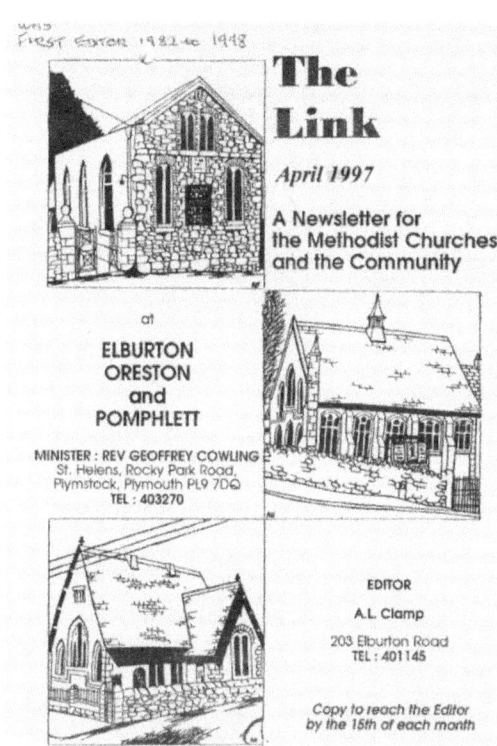

Community and Philanthropic Spirit

His commitment to serving others was evident in his long-standing involvement with the Elburton Methodist Church. He was the Sunday School Superintendent for over 15 years and served as the editor of the wider church's monthly newsletter, "The Link," for a similar duration. After Rosemary's very sad passing, Arthur later remarried and, following a chance encounter with a professor from India, established a connection with a missionary school in Chennai. Together with his new wife, Christine, he co-founded a "Sponsor a Child's Education" program that continues to this day.

Pictured left – The cover of 'The Link' complete with hand drawn sketches of each church by Angela
Below right – Arthur Clamp promoting his latest book
Below left – Arthur at home with his first wife, Rosemary
Below centre – Arthur on holiday with his second wife, Christine

A Legacy of Learning and Positivity

Arthur's greatest passion was history, which he brought to life through tireless research, documentation, and the many books he authored. He was driven by a need to "never be stuck in a rut," constantly seeking new experiences, meeting new people, and expanding his knowledge. With a positive attitude and a great sense of humour, he was always ready to help others, leaving a lasting impact on his family and community. His children, Susan, Angela, Elizabeth, David, and Steven, remember him with love and gratitude.

David Clamp, 2025

A Legacy of Local History

Below is the story of how Arthur L Clamp began writing books, in his own words, drafted shortly before he passed away in 2001. I have only made minor alterations to this text, correcting grammatical errors that he did not survive to correct himself. When I first discovered this text, I was shocked to see my name mentioned. It seems that, unbeknownst to me, I shared my first PC with him. I suspect he used it during the day when I was at school, although I do have one memory of sitting with him and showing him how it worked. It has been a pleasure to pick up where he left off and see his books republished and redistributed, and to know that I was part of the story, even back then. It was also fascinating to discover that his pricing structure matches the way I have tried to price the books, with a third going to local sellers and the rest covering printing costs with a little left over for my expenses.

I am his eldest grandson, and it is a privilege to curate his legacy, which we are calling 'The Clamp Collection'. The very last line of the text originally reads "The following pages list all the titles." Sadly, that page is missing and we have no record of all the books he published and knowing that some of those were researched by other authors makes the process of finding them even harder. I look forward to one day completing the collection and seeing them all available again. And maybe, one day, I'll even start writing my own to add to the series. For now, here is his story in his own words.

Steven Gibson, 2025

Writing and Publishing Booklets on Local Topics and Areas

I started this interest in either 1968 or 1969 when living in Woodford. I had by these dates established the Department of Printing and I think I must have been looking for something different to do. The first titles were of A5 size proofed from type set at Clarke, Doble and Brendon, Ltd., Plymouth printers, and then made up into pages and printed at Sawtell and Neilson, Ltd., Totnes.

Then began a slow process of getting them out to shops, etc. which proved to be more time consuming and difficult than actually researching, writing and getting the books into print. However, I persisted and opened a business account with Barclays Bank on the Broadway. I was advised to give it a title so I called it "Westway Publications". There came along another problem, one of storage of paper and finished books which was solved when the family moved to Elburton in 1970.

I changed the printer to Penwell, Ltd., Callington, Cornwall, as he was then just setting up himself and his prices seemed very reasonable. I did not get any of the printers to make up the complete books. I hand folded the flat printed sheets, stitched the books on a small manual table stitcher and trimmed them in a small hand turned guillotine which I bought from someone in Penzance for £40. It was brought up in a van.

The trouble and time going to and fro to Callington was too much so I transferred the printing to PDS Printers, Prince Rock, Plymouth, and I have been with them ever since. Now they are at Plympton which is easy to reach and they fold the flat sheets which was turning out to be a long chore which only saved a small part of the printing costs.

All my first titles were written by myself. I took the photographs and developed them in the loft of the house, the type was set by now on a computer situated in the house at Elburton from which I had collected photographic lengths of text to cut up and law down as pages.

At some point I decided that I would do my own film processing of lith film so I bought a large second hand process camera from Kingsbridge and learnt through trial and error to make line negatives of the text and halftone negatives of the illustrations which proved more difficult than I anticipated. The main problem was trying to keep the developer in the large dish at the correct temperature as any change would affect the developing time. I replaced this old camera with a brand new one bought from Croydon, Surrey, costing £900. This has turned out to be a great asset cutting out an expensive part of the printer's costs and one crucial aspect of the work which I could control.

By the middle 1970s there were many outlets I had contacted in Plymouth, up to Dartmoor, Exeter, around to Torbay, Totnes, Dartmouth and the South Hams. The market for local books was much greater than I had first thought and through getting to know many local people undertaking research themselves had the chance to help and make up books for other people who had in most instances, got together a collection of photographs with some text in a rather muddled way. Through my experience in print I was able to shape up their work and get it into print and in every case I had to pay the printer and let the person have the royalties. In the majority of titles produced in this manner this was another way of producing titles and it did give some profit to my work. However, I must say that in a few cases I lost out by either the other person getting the numbers wrong, not returning any monies from stock I delivered or they thought that more of their books should have been sold.

The print run was usually 1,000 copies and from time to time I have had reprints of 250 copies. It took about ten years to clear the first print run so I always had large stocks in the garage, workshop, etc. The numbers sold during the early years was about 7,000 copies a year increasing to around 9,000 copies and for the whole of the enterprise about 500,000 have been sold. The booklets have become part of the local scene and many people collect them, shops regularly order copies and I go around certain areas month by month restocking or replacing titles as necessary.

During the past year or so I have started setting the text on a Packard Bell PC, something which I should have done some years back. I share it with Steven Gibson, my grandson. There appears to be no end to the market for local books, but I could not earn a regular income because of the long time it takes to sell stock.

However, now exceeding 100 titles made up mainly of A4 twenty-four page booklets, some folded guides, with selling prices set with a third going to the shop which is the trade custom, the original idea has been quite successful and could go on for ever.

Apart from monetary benefits, however spasmodically these might be, I have learnt a lot myself, met many interesting people and have become part of the local scene with requests to give talks and to advise people about getting into print.

Arthur L Clamp, 2001

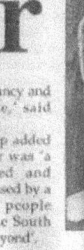

This newspaper article, published by the Evening Herald on 17th August 2001, forms a good record of his life. Just as he encourages us to learn more about local history, we encourage you to learn a little about him. For that reason, we have included these pages at the back of all the most recently republished books, in honour of his memory and recognition of his contribution to the community.

www.ingramcontent.com/pod-product-compliance
Lightning Source LLC
Chambersburg PA
CBHW061407070526
44584CB00031B/4182